First published 1994

ISBN 0 7110 2230 5

IAN ALLAN *Publishing*

Terminal House, Station Approach,
Shepperton, Surrey TW17 8AS.

INDUSTRIAL STEAM

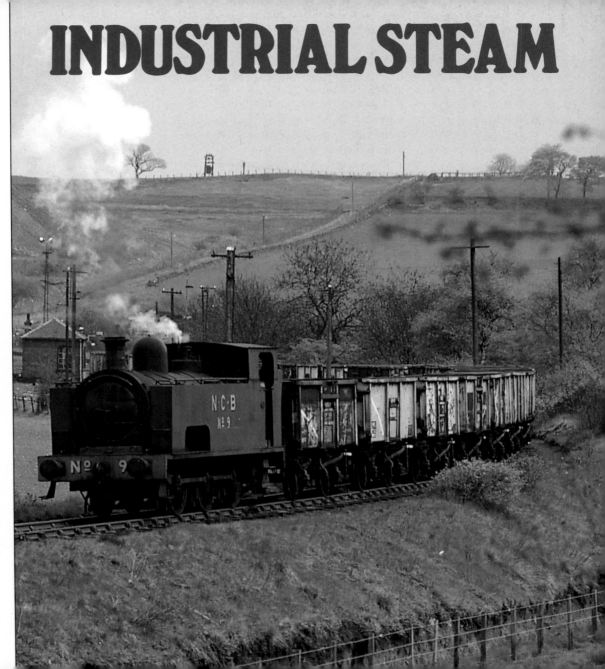

Front cover:
Wheldale Colliery, adjacent to the Sheffield-York main
line near Castleford in West Yorkshire, was the scene
of a remarkable return to working steam in December
1981, in order to test mechanical stoking equipment
built by Hunslet of Leeds and intended for export.
However, frost damage to Wheldale's diesels meant
that No 7 (Hunslet gas-produced 'Austerity' No 3168
of 1944) was kept going for several months rather than
the three-week testing period originally envisaged,
much to the delight of local railway photographers.
No 7 is seen shunting alongside the screens on 25 January 1982. The locomotive is now on display at the
Embsay Steam Railway. *Bob Avery*

Back cover:
Bradford Corporation once owned an extensive rail
system at its Esholt Sewage Works which was quite
photogenic — if you could cope with the rarified atmosphere! At the time of an Industrial Railway Society
visit on 24 April 1977, the last steam locomotive on
site, 1958-built Hudswell Clarke No 1888 0-4-0ST
Elizabeth looks resplendent in the morning sunshine.
Elizabeth is preserved at the Leeds Industrial Museum.
Tom Heavyside

Designed and printed by Ian Allan Printing Ltd, Coombelands
House, Coombelands Lane, Addlestone, Weybridge, Surrey
KT15 1HY.

Introduction

Although, without a doubt, main line steam was the glamorous end of railway operation, it was the myriad industrial lines which provided many of the most fascinating scenes of the steam locomotive at work.

From the earliest days of the steam locomotive, steam and industry were synonymous — after all the first working steam locomotives were to be found at industrial sites in the north, such as Wylam Colliery and the Middleton Railway — and industrial steam was, ultimately, to outlive steam on the main line by more than a decade.

Britain as 'The Workshop of the World' had founded its prosperity around coal and iron. Areas like the West Riding of Yorkshire, the Black Country, the northeast and Shropshire, where the coal and iron ore seams were closest to the surface, were amongst the earliest to witness the Industrial Revolution and, whilst the first industrial plateways were to be horse-powered, the lines thus created formed a natural basis for the later steam-operated railways.

In an age where virtually all freight — certainly most of what can be regarded as non-bulk traffic — is carried by the ubiquitous juggernaut, it is very easy to forget how important the steam locomotive was at even a small industrial site until comparatively recently. Brick works, breweries, docks and harbours, cement works, chemical works and power stations, as well as the more obvious collieries and iron works, all played host to intricate networks of industrial railways. Examine in detail a large scale

Previous page:
Bedlay Colliery, Glenboig, Lanarkshire, just north of Coatbridge, became the penultimate colliery, and the last in Scotland, to use steam when it closed on 9 December 1982. NCB No 9, a Hudswell Clarke 0-6-0T No 895 of 1909 vintage, is seen here shunting loaded wagons slowly over the weighbridge, before hauling them to the BR exchange sidings on 15 May 1978.
Tom Heavyside

Left:
The Craig Merthyr-Pontardulais system was without doubt the most scenic British line to continue with genuine steam into the 1970s. The line rose steeply to the tiny colliery nestling on the very edge of the Brecon Beacons, and two or sometimes three return trips were made most weekday mornings. As well as serving the colliery, the trains were used as unofficial distributors of newspapers and provisions to the inhabitants of isolated cottages near the line. Here Bagnall 'Austerity' 0-6-0ST (2758/1944) leaves Craig Merthyr Colliery with loads for the exchange sidings on 26 May 1978, just weeks before the closure of both colliery and railway. The Bagnall is now preserved at Leamington Spa.

Derek Huntriss

Ordnance Survey map of a place like Burton-on-Trent and suddenly it becomes clear how large these networks could be and how far a map delineating purely the main line railways distorts the reality on the ground. In places, such as the northeast (with the various lines around Ashington) and in the Fife coalfield, the pre-Nationalisation coal owners constructed huge networks of lines that could more than compete with the lines owned by some of the biggest of the pre-Grouping companies.

For the steam enthusiast the industrial lines of Britain could prove fascinating. Small, often elderly, tank engines struggled day-in-day-out to operate in the most difficult of environments; heavily graded lines, poorly maintained and lightly engineered, were the order of the day and the trains often comprised an interesting collection of decrepit and aged rolling stock.

To provide the motive power for the various industrial lines a whole industry grew up. Engine building became centred in places like Leeds — with Hunslet, Hudwell Clarke, Kitson and Manning Wardle — and Bristol — with Peckett and Avonside — that were well away from the traditional 'railway towns'. Although these companies could, and did, construct locomotives for the main line companies their bread and butter was the supply of relatively small tank engines for industrial concerns — and what a business it could prove to be at the height of the railway age. By the time that the company ceased production in the early 1960s, the northeast firm of Robert Stephenson & Hawthorns had constructed more than 8,000 locomotives — the majority of which were steam powered. Other companies too, like Hunslet, could number their products in thousands.

But just as steam on the main line was gradually to disappear, so too was steam in industry. Diesel traction was to be equally attractive in industry as it was to British Rail and the decline in industrial steam was exacerbated by the steady decline, from the 1950s onwards, of the traditional heavy industries that required railway connections. As steel works and iron stone quarries disappeared, as coal mines became exhausted, as the ship yards gradually succumbed to the pressures of competition from the Far East, so the railways associated with them also ceased to operate. But industrial steam struggled on through the 1970s and even into

the 1980s. No doubt, even in the 1990s, the occasional foray of steam on to an industrial system will be reported in the railway press but, to all intents, 'real' industrial steam has finally died.

Of course, it is still possible to recreate the atmosphere of an industrial environment to a certain extent — witness the preserved sections of the Tanfield, Bowes and Sittingbourne Railways — and numerous industrial locomotives also survive, but the reality of the preserved lines is subtly different to the reality of industrial environment. We hope that this selection of illustrations portraying 'real' industrial steam illustrates colourfully a now departed facet of Britain's railway history.

Credits
We would like to thank the following photographers who have allowed us to use their material in this book: Bob Avery, Brian Dobbs, Tom Heavyside, Derek Huntriss, Geoff Lumb, Keith Pirt and Ron White (of Colour Rail).

Right:
Locomotives that worked on the Lambton, Hetton & Joicey colliery system were instantly recognisable by their uniquely shaped cab roofs. RSH-built 0-6-2T (works No 3377 of 1909) climbs away from Hetton washery in February 1969. As NCB No 5 fights to keep its feet the sun, deep snow and steam help create a superb scene which preservation cannot hope to achieve.
Colour Rail/C. A. Davies (IR72)

5

Left:
Aveling & Porter was responsible for a handful of unique traction engine-based geared locomotives, this example was built in 1906 for the Mountfield Gypsum Mine Tramway. *Sirapite* (6158/1906) is seen here going about its domestic duties at Richard Garrett's works at Leiston, Suffolk, where it was quite capable of working the 1 in 37 incline to the works. Garretts were well known for the own traction engine designs and one wonders why they did not build their 'own' shunter. The 'long shop', one of the earliest production line assembly halls in existence, is now a museum featuring over 200 years of Garrett's works. *Siraphite* is now privately preserved at Wellington.
Colour Rail (IR119)

Above:
This 2-2-0TG (works No 9449 built in 1926) was another Aveling & Porter-built enigma. Seen on 22 June 1963 at the Associated Portland Cement Holborough Works, Snodland. Cement works were characterised by the colour of the surrounding area. This locomotive is now in full working order and based on the Bluebell line.
Geoff Lumb

Left:
Edward Lloyds paper mills (later Bowaters United Kingdom Paper Mills Co Ltd) at Sittingbourne Kent had a 2ft 6in gauge network that linked the various parts of the complex together. Pictured here is 0-4-4-0T *Monarch* on 22 June 1963; the unusual design of chimney was to prevent spark throwing, an essential fitting for a paper works locomotive. The locomotive was built by Bagnall in 1953 (works No 3024). On the closure of the Bowaters' railway network in October 1969 a section passed to the Locomotive Club of Great Britain for preservation as the Sittingbourne & Kemsley Light Railway and a number of locomotives can still be seen on home territory; *Monarch* , originally preserved at Welshpool, is now on the Ffestiniog Railway, where it is being converted to the Welsh line's 1ft ½ gauge.
Geoff Lumb

Above:
0-6-2Ts at rest between duties; *Chevallier* and *Conqueror* (Manning Wardle works Nos 1877 of 1915 and Bagnall 2192 of 1922) are seen between duties at Ridham Dock on the 22 June 1963. Both still exist and earn their keep on the Great Whipsnade Railway.
Geoff Lumb

Left:
Built in 1949 by Robert Stephenson & Hawthorns (Works No 7544) 0-4-0ST *Bonnie Prince Charlie* is seen at Corralls Ltd, Hamworthy, Railway Wharf, Poole Harbour on 1 June 1963. This particular locomotive is now preserved at the Great Western Society at Didcot.
Geoff Lumb

Right:
The dumpy profile of Bagnall-built 0-4-0ST No 3058 of 1953 *Alfred* is clearly seen at English China Clay's Port of Par in St Austell Bay, Cornwall, on 15 June 1977. There were five miles of sidings and a loading gauge of 7ft 6in caused by the need to negotiate a very low bridge necessitated locomotives of short stature. *Alfred* now resides, not far from its original haunts, on the Bodmin & Wentford Railway.
Tom Heavyside

Left:
National Coal Board veteran 0-6-0ST, built at the
Peckett & Sons Ltd, Atlas Locomotive Works, Bristol
in 1916, works No 1426, is employed at Brynlliw
Colliery landsdale yard, Grovesend, near Llanelli,
South Wales on 20 September 1979. Retirement
followed at the Swansea Industrial & Maritime
Museum.
Tom Heavyside

Right:
This locomotive was built for the Great Western
Railway in 1929 by the North British Locomotive Co
(Works No 24042). Numbered 7754 it is seen in March
1968 having been sold into industrial service by British
Railways. The photograph shows it heading a 'paddy
train' from Talywain to Blaenserchen. The locomotive
was worked into the ground by the NCB, and following
its failure was left to rot away for a number of years
before transfer to the Llangollen Railway for
restoration.
Derek Huntriss

Left:
Avonside Engine Co built this 0-6-0ST in 1914 as works No 1680, and some years later got the contract for a rebuild. Named *Sir John* it is seen here in March 1969 while in service at Mountain Ash Colliery, near Aberdare, in South Wales.
Derek Huntriss

Above:
Some 12 years later, on 1 July 1981, *Sir John* lies discarded by the NCB in the yard at Mountain Ash. This locomotive still exists, preserved at the Vale of Neath Railway Society headquarters at Aberdulais.
Tom Heavyside

Left:
Ex-Cadbury Brothers Ltd, Bournville, this Avonside 0-4-0T (works No 1977/1925) is seen on 18 October 1965 as originally preserved at the Dowty Railway Centre, Ashchurch. Later the locomotive saw service on the Gloucestershire-Warwickshire Railway before moving closer to 'home' at the Birmingham Railway Museum, Tyseley.
Geoff Lumb

Above:
National Coal Board, West Midlands Area No 2 at Cannock Chase's colliery was this 1889-built Hudswell Clarke 0-6-0T, works No 319. *Stafford i*s pictured at Cannock Wood, Rawsley, Hednesford on 23 September 1963.
Geoff Lumb

Left:
1899-built 0-6-0ST, Peckett works No 786, No 3 *Progress* is pictured on 23
September 1963 with a 'paddy' train to Hednesford while working for the National
Coal Board West Midlands area No 2 at Cannock Chase on 23 September 1963.
Geoff Lumb

Above:
Alders Paper Mills Ltd at Tamworth operated this Andrew Barclay 0-6-0ST,
(1576/1918) with spark arrestor. It is pictured on 23 September 1963.
Geoff Lumb

Left:
The sight of a Beyer-Garrett was not exactly common in Great Britain, therefore to see an example going about its everyday duty as late as June 1961 was something to behold. Sneyd Colliery No 3, an 0-4-0+0-4-0 example, in maroon livery is seen passing a McKenzie & Holland signal with a rake of empties in tow. A similar machine, *William Francis*, worked at Baddesley Colliery prior to preservation at Bressingham Steam Museum.
Colour Rail/J. P. Mullett (IR63)

Above:
Loddington Ironstone Quarries, worked by the Loddington Ironstone Co Ltd, was another site of iron ore in Northamptonshire. Bagnall 0-6-0ST (Works No 2655), built in 1941, *Loddington No 2* is pictured at work in the quarry on 25 September 1961.
Geoff Lumb

Left:
One of those industries that has been largely forgotten in Britain in recent years is the extraction of iron ore. Huge areas of counties like Northamptonshire were once exploited for this essential raw material of the Industrial Revolution. *Pitsford*, an 0-6-0ST built by the Avonside Engine Co of Bristol in 1923 (Works No 1917), is seen approaching the BR exchange sidings, situated close to Pitsford & Brampton station on the ex-LNWR route from Northampton to Market Harborough, whilst working at Pitsford Ironstone Quarries on 25 September 1961. The locomotive is now preserved at Steamtown (Carnforth).
Geoff Lumb

Above:
A beautiful view of one of the three metre-gauge Peckett locomotives operated by Stewart & Lloyds Minerals Ltd, Wellingborough Quarries on 25 September 1961. All three of these little Pecketts managed to survive the general slaughter that most ironstone systems suffered from and can be seen at the Irchester Narrow Gauge Railway Museum, just south of Wellingborough.
Geoff Lumb

Far left:
Kettering Furnaces No 6, at work on the 3ft gauge track of the Kettering Iron & Coal Co Ltd, a subsidiary of Stewarts & Lloyds. This 0-6-OST 3ft 0in gauge locomotive was built by Manning Wardle (works No 1123) in 1889, and survives to this day at Market Harborough. No 6 was one of three similar locomotives delivered between then and 1906 for operation over the extensive network of lines serving the Northamptonshire iron and steel industry.
Geoff Lumb

Left:
The driver of *Kettering Furnaces No 3* keeps an eye open for trouble as his Black Hawthorne-built 0-4-0ST (859 of 1885) propels a rake of tub wagons, June 1960. Kettering mainly used the Black Hawthorn locomotives for shunting purposes, whilst the Manning Wardles were used on the 'main line' services. No 3 survived the line's closure to be preserved at Penrhyn Castle Museum.
ColourRail (IR113)

Above:
As well as a brace of Black Hawthorns, Kettering also kept this Manning Wardle (1370 of 1897) busy. *Kettering Furnaces No 7* is seen at Rothwell Pit with a rake of wooden tub wagons in the process of being filled. This timeless scene was taken in June 1960, two years before operations ceased.
ColourRail (IR114)

Left:
Built by Black Hawthorn in 1879 (works No 501) this locomotive saw many years service hauling ironstone at Kettering. Viewed in 1959 *Kettering Furnaces No 2* did not survive the end of steam on the line.
Colour Rail (IR112)

Above:
Seen outside the depot of the Nassington Barrowden Mining Co Ltd *Jacks Green* and *Ring Haw* were photographed in their last month of operation, December 1970. The Hunslet Engine Co built *Jacks Green* for the opening of the quarry in 1939, with *Ring Haw* following in 1940 (works Nos 1953 and 1982). The photographer's 1938 Series 2 Morris 8, is posed alongside the locomotives, both of which survive in preservation.
Derek Huntriss

Left:
Pictured during March 1963 is Andrew Barclay 0-4-0CT works No 855 of 1899 *Stanton No 10* a three-ton crane tank belonging to Stanton & Staveley Ltd at Stanton Ironworks near Ilkeston, Derbyshire.
Geoff Lumb

Above:
On 4 October 1963 Robert Stephenson & Hawthorns No 53 is seen working at Stewarts & Lloyd Minerals Ltd's Corby Ironstone Quarries. Note the iron ore in the wagons; the Corby steel works was provided for many years with iron ore quarried from local sources. To link the quarries with the furnaces an intricate network of lines was constructed — both standard and narrow gauge — which have almost entirely disappeared. No 53 was built in 1941 (works No 7030). Whilst this particular locomotive has subsequently been scrapped, sister locomotive No 54 (RSH 7031/1941) is now preserved at the East Anglian Railway Museum at Chappel & Wakes Colne station.
Geoff Lumb

Left:
The Rutland Railway Museum is now home to this 1912-built Peckett 0-4-0ST (works No 1257). Seen outside the engine shed at its previous 'home' in May 1967, *Uppingham* was owned by Tarmac Roadstone Holdings Ltd and worked at their Wirksworth Limestone Quarry.
Derek Huntriss

Above:
Winifred, one of the many small Hunslet-built 0-4-0STs, pauses between shunting duties on the 1st Level at Penrhyn quarries in August 1958. In June 1966 *Winifred*, along with a number of other locomotives was exported to the United States for preservation.
Keith Pirt/K. R. Photographics (C62)

Left:
Amongst the multitude of 'Baby' Hunslets at the Penrhyn Quarries was this Andrew Barclay-built 0-4-0T *Cegin* (1991/1931); it was acquired secondhand from the Durham County Water Board, Wearhead, in October 1936. It is seen here resting between shunting duties complete with an improvised 'shunters' truck.
Keith Pirt/K. R. Photographics (C127)

Right:
Hunslet-built 0-4-0ST *Linda* is seen on the Port Penrhyn main line in August 1958 hauling a train of empties at one of the intermediate crossing loops.
Keith Pirt/K. R. Photographics (C61)

Above:
The works area at Port Penrhyn was well known for its line-up of locomotives awaiting overhaul, or disposal. This line up in August 1958, includes *Lilian* (Hunslet 317/1883) now preserved at Launceston.
Keith Pirt/K. R. Photographics (C130)

Right:
Linda lounges on the dockside, alongside the tramp steamer *Sir W. Campbell.* In this August 1958 view an air of dereliction is already descending over the port area, as witnessed by the grass growing unchecked.
Keith Pirt/K. R. Photographics (C174)

Left:
No 41708, a Midland Railway-built 0-6-0T is pictured on 23 September 1962 whilst on loan to Staveley Coal & Iron Co. The company had a 100-year agreement with the Midland Railway (and its successors) to supply motive power which resulted in five S. W. Johnson-designed MR Class 1F 0-6-0TS still being in service until expiry of the agreement in 1965. No 41708 was one of three locomotives supplied under this agreement, resulting in its subsequent preservation by the Midland 1F Society, and now based at Swanage.
Geoff Lumb

Above:
This somewhat ancient, but exquisite-looking 0-6-0ST was built by Beyer-Peacock (works No 1830) in 1870, and rebuilt by the Yorkshire Engine Co in 1910. As Rothervale No 0 (unusual in itself) it is seen bathed in the warm sunshine at Treeton in April 1958.
Colour Rail (IR116)

Above:
A superb general view of the Doxford & Sunderland Shipbuilding & Engineering Co's engine shed in May 1968; showing, from left to right, *Millfield, Southwick, Hendon, Roker* and *General*, the latter a Peckett product. The first four are RSH-built 0-4-0 crane tanks. These locomotives were extremely useful beasts in a heavy engineering environment as they possessed steam-operated jibs with three fixed position hooks and as such had capacity to lift and transport heavy items around the shipyard. All four of these crane tanks were subsequently preserved.
Colour Rail (IR114)

Right:
Hendon (RSH 7007/1940) bathes in the sunshine outside the shed at Doxford on 16 April 1969. *Hendon* survived to be preserved at the Tanfield Railway.
Dr P. Ravenscroft/K. R. Photographics (C183)

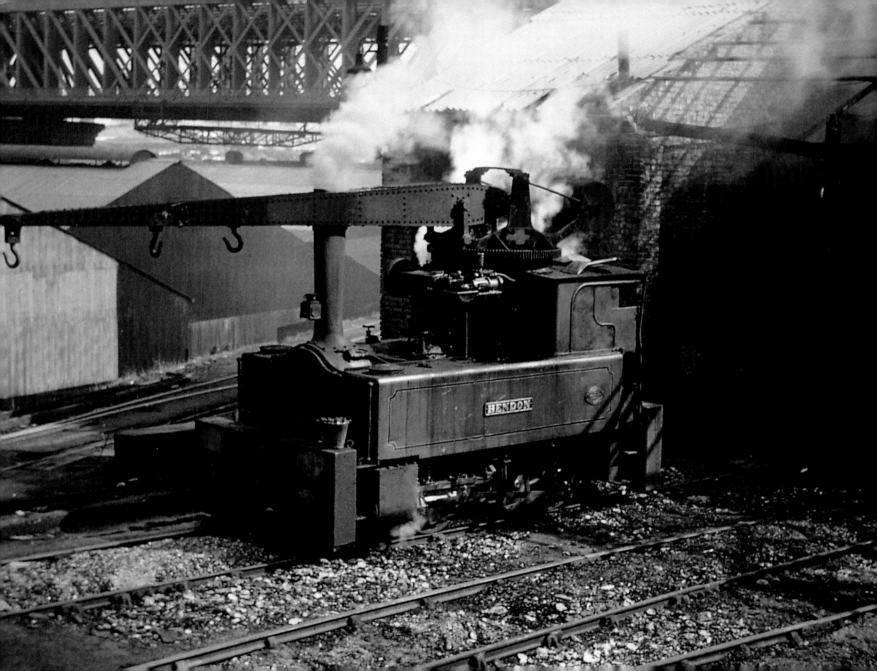

Above:
Woolley Colliery is situated just north of Darton on the ex-Lancashire & Yorkshire Railway line from Horbury to Barnsley. *Woolley No 2* 0-6-0ST, built in 1898, is seen working in the colliery, part of the NCB's North Eastern Division, on 26 September 1961. The locomotive, built by Hudswell Clarke works No 486 is seen against a back drop of pit-head winding gear.
Geoff Lumb

Right:
In the NCB's South Yorkshire area was Harworth Colliery, here No 1 (YEC) attempts to haul the preserved Gresley 'N2' Class 0-6-2T No 69523 out of the engine shed in November 1963.
Keith Pirt/K. R. Photographics (C209)

Left:
Built at the London & South Western Railway's workshops at Nine Elms in 1892 this Class B4 0-4-0T, saw service with the LSWR and later the Southern Railway before being sold into industrial service in 1949. Sold to the Ministry of Fuel & Power, SR No 92 is seen at Wm Pepper & Co, Darton Screening Plant, near Wakefield on 2 April 1960. No 92 survived in service until the summer of 1961 when it was cut up for scrap.
Geoff Lumb

Right:
Nunnery Colliery at Sheffield with Hawthorn Leslie (879 of 1911), an outside cylinder 0-6-0T, hustling about the yard in October 1956.
Keith Pirt/K. R. Photographics (C63)

Left:
Nunnery Colliery this time at Blast Lane wharf, Sheffield, after bringing coal trucks down for barge shipment in September 1958.
Keith Pirt/K. R. Photographics (C289)

Above:
Seen on 4 May 1963 at Acton Hall Colliery, near Featherstone in West Yorkshire, is the National Coal Board's North East Division's 0-6-0ST No S.106 *Airedale*. The locomotive, works No 1440, was constructed by Hunslet in 1923. This is one of many industrial steam locomotives that have found a home in preservation at the Embsay Steam Railway.
Geoff Lumb

44

Left:
During 1960/61 the Hunslet Engine Co Ltd developed an underfed stoker and gas producer system in an effort to improve the efficiency of steam locomotives and to reduce the incidence of black smoke following the 1956 Clean Air Act. Engines fitted with the equipment could readily be distinguished by a conical shaped chimney — which did nothing to enhance their appearance as seen here on NCB No 5134 Hunslet 'Austerity' 0-6-0ST No 3168 built in 1944. In steam's twilight hours in autumn 1981 surprisingly Hunslet instigated further tests with the equipment fitted to No 5134 using different grades of coal, first steamed at Wheldale Colliery, adjacent to the Sheffield-York main line near Castleford, West Yorkshire, where longer runs were possible on trips to Fryston Colliery. No 5134 is depicted at Fryston Colliery during the trials on the biting cold morning of 10 December 1981.
Tom Heavyside

Above:
Wheldale's 'Austerity' found a week's work in June 1982 working the NCB-owned line between Wheldale and nearby Fryston Colliery. Here driver Colin Davies eases No 7 away from Wheldale amongst a pleasing variety of flora with another train of coal for blending and washing on the 17th of the month. Historians of railway wagons will no doubt find much of interest in the assortment of vehicles marshalled behind the locomotive.
Bob Avery

Right:
All good things come to an end and before Hunslet 'Austerity' No 3168 departed from Wheldale, for pastures new on the Yorkshire Dales Railway — now Emsbay Steam Railway, near Skipton — some final steamings were arranged in September 1982. With a suitable Wheldale Farewell headboard above the smokebox No 5134 pays its last respects to Fryston Colliery before its final journey back to Wheldale Colliery on 24 September 1982.
Tom Heavyside

Above:
1935 0-6-0ST *Jubilee* Hunslet-built works No 1725 is seen at Allerton Bywater in the NCB's North Eastern Division No 8 Castleford area is seen during April 1962.
Geoff Lumb

Right
In December 1981, Hunslet 0-6-0 ST (3168/1944) shunts the yard at Wheldale Colliery, Near Castleford, Yorkshire. This locomotive, alias NCB No 7, had lain out of use for several years at the nearby colliery at Allerton Bywater. At the time, the Hunslet Engine Company was experimenting with new designs of mechanical stoking equipment for general industrial use and were looking around for a suitable test bed to evaluate its equipment. No 7 appeared to fit the test criteria admirably, and it was removed from store and diesel hauled to Wheldale, over BR tracks via Wakefield Kirkgate, where it was put into steam after arrival in November 1981.
Brian Dobbs

Left:
Once the razzamatazz of 'Rocket 150' in May 1980 had died away steam carried on in intermittent use at Bold until September 1982. Much of the traffic was bound for export via Garston docks, and was moved in modern HEA coal hoppers. Here *Robert* (Hudswell Clarke 'Austerity' 0-6-0ST No 1752 of 1943) moves a colourful rake of these vehicles into position for loading on a perfect winter's morning on 24 February 1982. On 23 September of that year, *Robert* (now preserved at Crewe) worked the last steam turn at Bold. The following day, Wheldale's Hunslet No 7 (3168/1944) worked its last shift, bringing to a close regular steam operation in British industry.
Bob Avery

Left:
The emergence of No 7 and its return to steam was a great surprise for enthusiasts and the Wheldale staff. The locomen at Wheldale certainly appeared to welcome the opportunity, and challenge, of keeping steam alive, and certainly, the Hunslet looked at home amidst the pithead gear and spoil heaps. The locomotive was mostly used on the runs down to the stockpiles alongside the barge wharves on the River Aire, although it did make the occasional foray down the line to the adjacent Fryston Colliery. During the big freeze of January and February 1982, which wreaked havoc with the Colliery's diesel fleet, No 7 was in daily use until it was demoted to standby use in March 1982. However, it was put back in use again in July, mainly working the Fryston shuttle, before finally bowing out in the autumn. On 11 November 1982, the 'Austerity' left Wheldale by road for its new home at the Embsay Steam Railway where it is kept in immaculate condition and full working order. Over a decade later, although No 7 still survives, its old stamping grounds at Wheldale, Fryston and Allerton Bywater have all disappeared in the name of progress.
Brian Dobbs

Right:
Just out of sight to the left in this photograph taken at Bold Colliery, adjacent to the Liverpool & Manchester main line near St Helens in Lancashire, are numerous preserved steam locomotives gathered together for the 'Rocket 150' celebrations at Rainhill in May 1980. Despite the splendour and charisma of so many magnificent locomotives, daily life goes on. Amazingly ignored by the vast majority of the numerous photographers present, 'Austerity' 0-6-0ST *Joseph*, built by Hunslet in 1944 (Works No 3163), moves empty 16-ton wagons towards the screen on 22 May 1980. This particular locomotive was rebuilt by Hunslet in 1965 (works No 3885) and is currently stored at the closed Chatterley Whitfield mining museum in Staffordshire.
Bob Avery

Left:
Hudswell Clarke 0-4-0ST *Mirvale* is now one of the most familiar industrial locomotives in preservation, having been based originally on the North Yorkshire Moors Railway and most recently on the Gwili. Built by the Leeds-based company in 1955 (works No 1885) for the Mirvale Chemical Co Ltd of Mirfield, West Yorkshire, the locomotive is seen at its original home on 14 October 1961.
Geoff Lumb

Above:
North Eastern Gas Board 0-4-0ST (Andrew Barclay works No 1783 of 1922), nicknamed the 'Beaumont Street Flyer', steams towards the Midland Goods Yard in Huddersfield with a train of empty coke wagons on 30 June 1962. Note the overhead wiring for the town's trolleybus system.

Above:
Imperial Chemical Industries Ltd, Dyedstuffs division at Dalton Works, Huddersfield owned, this 0-4-0ST built in 1946 seen carrying its works number, 2226, on the tank side. The three-man crew pose for their picture to be taken on 4 November 1961,

little wondering that some 30 years later their charge would be a static exhibit in Penrhyn Castle Museum.
Geoff Lumb

Below:
Perhaps one of the most unlikely spots to find steam locomotives still working into the 1980s was at Crossley's scrapyard in Shipley, West Yorkshire. The yard was adjacent to Shipley station and rail connected to the BR line from Bradford Forster Square. The diminutive Barclay-built 0-4-0ST *Harry* was employed on internal shunting duties and was certainly at home amidst the piles of scrap metal awaiting recycling. *Harry* was rescued for preservation and is now at the Pontypool & Bleanavon Railway. (It also spent time at Peak Rail and Middleton Railway). *Brian Dobbs*

Left:
Peckett 0-6-0ST *Nonslip Stone* (works No 2160 of 1956) is seen at Brooks Ltd's Chemical Works at Lightcliff near Halifax on 1 May 1962. This locomotive was one of the last industrial steam locomotives to be constructed by the Bristol-based company of Peckett. In the same year as No 2160 was built the company also produced two prototype diesel locomotives, but Peckett was not to achieve great success in this field and production ceased completely in 1959. The last steam locomotive built, works No 2165, was a 3ft gauge engine destined for Mozambique.
Geoff Lumb

Above:
Another view of *Nonslip Stone* at Brook's Lightcliffe, Halifax, this time pictured on 18 December 1964. The tipping wagon is doing its best to over power the locomotive.
Geoff Lumb

Above:
Built in 1914 by Manning Wardle — another of the Leeds-based locomotive builders — 0-6-0ST *Success* (works No 1844) gleams outside the National Coal Board's North Eastern Division's Newmarket Silkstone Colliery at Stanley. In the late 1950s there were a total of 17 collieries served by rail in the NCB's No 8 Castleford area. The locomotive is pictured on 5 May 1963.
Geoff Lumb

Right:
Head Wrightson 0-4-0VBT (works No 21/1870) is seen on 19 September 1965 at the Teesdale Ironworks at Thornaby-on-Tees, in the North Riding of Yorkshire. It was originally built in 1870 for Seaham Harbour Dock Ltd, Seaham Harbour, Co Durham. At this time the locomotive was already preserved. It is now to be found at Preston Hall.
Geoff Lumb

Above:
Agecroft Power Station lay alongside the ex-Lancashire & Yorkshire Manchester-Bolton main line, and its small fleet of Robert Stephenson & Hawthorn 0-4-0STs could normally be glimpsed from passing trains. The locomotives' duties were not arduous, involving moving rafts of loaded 16-ton wagons along, one at a time, as they were tipped. Nevertheless, it was the real thing, and on 2 June 1977 the photographer was able to talk his way past the security guard at the main entrance to get this shot of one of the three locomotives waiting patiently for tipping to commence.
Bob Avery

Right:
During the 1970s the Central Electricity Generating Board's Agecroft Power Station, in the Manchester suburbs, and situated close to the site of the former BR engine shed (26B), was one of the last commercial users of steam locomotives. Based here were three 0-4-0STs built by Robert Stephenson & Hawthorns although latterly they were only used spasmodically when the power station was buying coal other than from the adjacent NCB Agecroft Colliery. The former required shunting from the BR exchange sidings to the tippler, while Agecroft coal was fed directly by conveyor belt. Awaiting its next call to duty by the coaling stage outside the shed on 12 March 1977 is *Agecroft No 1*, RSH No 7416 built 1948. *Agecroft No 1* is now at the Fulstow Steam Centre, near Louth, Lincolnshire.
Tom Heavyside

Far right:
To mark the end of the railway system at Agecroft Power Station, Manchester, a 'Farewell to Steam' weekend was held, visitors enjoying rides in replica Liverpool & Manchester Railway coaches. For the occasion the three resident locomotives rejoiced in different liveries of green, blue and red, a stark contrast to those sported in previous years. On Saturday 12 September 1981 the youngest of the Robert Stephenson & Hawthorns trio of 0-4-0STs *Agecroft No 3* built in 1951, RSH No 7681 stands against a backdrop of impressive chimneys. In more recent times *Agecroft No 3* has seen regular use at the Greater Manchester Science & Railway Museum, Liverpool Road, Manchester.
Tom Heavyside

Above:
Many happy hours were spent by photographers at Lancashire's Bickershaw
Colliery, where from 1968 until 1979, and then intermittently until 1983, it was
possible momentarily to forget that the genuine working steam locomotive was a rare
beast in the British Isles. Bickershaw providxed almost continuous steam action
around the clock until the delivery of replacement diesels in 1979. Most days saw
two locomotives in steam, and on 2 June 1977 0-6-0ST No 8 (Hunslet 3776/1952)
pauses briefly between duties, alongside the infamous spoil heap. This locomotive
was later painted lined-out blue and named *Bickershaw* — as illustrated elsewhere in
this book. On withdrawal No 8 was to pass to the East Lancashire Railway for
preservation.
Bob Avery

Right:
A rare burst of winter sunshine catches Hunslet 'Austerity' 0-6-0ST No 8
(3776/1952) as it propels MGR empties towards the screens at Bickershaw on
10 February 1978. In the eight months since the photographer's previous encounter
with this locomotive, lined-blue livery and the name *Bickershaw* have been applied.
Bob Avery

Above:
'Austerity' 0-6-0STs *Respite* (left) built by Hunslet in 1950 as No 3696 and *Gwyneth*, a Robert Stephenson & Hawthorns example, No 7135 of 1944, have a forlorn look at Bickersaw Colliery, Leigh, Lancashire, on 5 September 1979, having been supplanted by a diesel locomotive. However for both 'Austerities' this was not the end, for after nearly 30 years of hard work in the Lancashire and West Cumberland coalfields, *Respite* subsequently found a safe haven at the National Railway Museum, York. Meanwhile parts of *Gwyneth* were used in the construction of the broad gauge replica *Iron Duke* — also normally based at the NRM.
Tom Heavyside

Right:
Bickershaw Colliery was situated in the industrial heartland of Lancashire, midway between the towns and mill chimneys of Wigan and Leigh, and in the later 1970s was perhaps an unlikely destination for British steam enthusiasts to head for. The attraction for many though was the NCB's fleet of ubiquitous 'Austerity' 0-6-0 ST which were engaged in frequent activity that could rival pre-1968 steam action. To the enthusiast, Bickershaw could offer action *par excellence*, with wonderful smoke scapes and the sound effects to match, and in its steam heyday could turn out locomotives in a variety of liveries. Steam was still in use at the colliery into the 80s, and green liveried Bickershaw No 7 (3776/1952) climbs away from the screens with a train-loaded HAAs for the BR exchange sidings. *Brian Dobbs*

Left:
Ex-LMS No 2271 0-6-2T *North Stafford No 2* is seen on 9 March 1965 leaving the yard at Mosley Common on the NCB's Walkden system near Manchester. Built by the North Staffordshire Railway at its Stoke Works in 1923 to a design of Adams, the locomotive, withdrawn in 1939, was one of several ex-NSR engines to pass into industrial use prior to Nationalisation. This locomotive had been named *Princess* until repainted in NSR livery in 1960. The locomotive, owned by the National Railway Museum, is in the care of the North Staffordshire Railway at Cheddleton.
Geoff Lumb

Right:
On 2 July 1960 the National Coal Board's North Western Division No 1 Manchester area's 0-8-0T *Emanuel Clegg* is pictured. *Emanual Clegg* was built in 1924 by Nasmyth Wilson and was one of two 0-8-OTs with Walschaerts valve gear bought by the Astley & Tyldesly Collieries Co for the Gin Pit railway system. The locomotive had ceased regular service in 1958 and was scrapped in 1965.
Geoff Lumb

Left:
National Coal Board, North Western Division No 2 Wigan area 0-6-0ST, ex-LMS 11456, Beyer Peacock works No 1989 was built in 1881 and rebuilt at Horwich in 1896. 11456 is pictured at Wigan Junction, Ince Moss Colliery during June 1961.
Geoff Lumb

Right:
National Coal Board, North Western Division Southfield area's 0-6-0WT works reference 'C', built in 1874 *Bellerophon* is seen at Lea Green Colliery in 1966 two years after it ceased work. This unusual-looking locomotive was built by Richard Evans & Co at Haydock Foundry for work on the company's own colliery lines and until 1948 passed for operation over main line metals between Earlestown and Warrington, prior to its preservation on the Keighley & Worth Valley Railway. The outside Gooch valve gear and piston valves are of particular interest.
Geoff Lumb

Above:
Hudswell Clarke 0-4-0ST (works No 1799) *Ribblesdale No 4* built in 1947 is seen in steam at Ribblesdale Cement Ltd, Clitheroe on 5 May 1962. Although later dieselised the works is associated with the sole-surviving BR Clayton Class 17 to be preserved — an unusual choice for an industrial shunter.
Geoff Lumb

Right:
On 27 May 1967 R. & W. Hawthorn Leslie-built 0-4-0ST, works No 3890 of 1936, *Helen* is seen parked outside the ramshackle engine shed at Sir Hedworth Williamson's Limeworks Ltd, Hartley Quarry, Kirkby Stephen.
Geoff Lumb

Left:
National Coal Board Northern Division, Ashington Colliery, RSH-built 0-6-0T, works No 7764 of 1954. Numbered 39 it is seen here with two North Eastern and one Furness Railway coach in tow along with eight wagons on special tour during June 1961. Note the variety of NCB internal wagons on show.
Geoff Lumb

Above:
On 16 June 1962 0-4-0ST No 27, built in 1918 by Hudswell Clarke (works No 1338), is pictured at National Coal Board North Eastern Division's Elsecar Colliery.
Geoff Lumb

Left:
RSH-built 0-4-0ST works No 7009 built in 1940 is seen here on 29 May 1965 at Millom Ironworks, Millom Hematite Ore and Iron Co Ltd. No 2 is unusual for an industrial locomotive in carrying its running number on a cabside plate.
Geoff Lumb

Above:
The larger users of industrial engines were accomplished engineers and the overhaul or rebuilding of locomotives posed few problems. No 2 was rebuilt at Newbattle in 1931, and is pictured on 19 July 1966 whilst working for the National Coal Board in the Scottish South Area at Lady Victoria Colliery, Newton Graves, Midlothian.
Geoff Lumb

Above:
Built in 1910, this Barclay 0-4-0ST, works No 1116, *West Ayr Area No 16* is seen working in the National Coal Board's Scottish South Area on 18 July 1966. The building on the right probably housed shunters between duties.
Geoff Lumb

Right:
National Coal Board Scottish south area's 0-6-0ST *Lothian's Area No 21*. Andrew Barclay's works No 2026, built in 1937, is pictured at Nidris Colliery on 19 July 1966.
Geoff Lumb

Left:
National Coal Board Scottish South Area Barclay 0-4-0ST (1007/1904) No 22 with an unidentified 0-6-0T cowering behind at Polkemmet Colliery on 19 July 1966. *Geoff Lumb*

Above:
Bedlay Colliery, despite being just a few miles from the centre of Glasgow, occupied a scenic setting in the foothills of the Campsie Fells. The action always occurred around dawn, which meant that an overnight drive along the M6/A74 was usually necessary for the photographer in order to find the railway working. Here Andrew Barclay 0-4-0ST (2296/1956) climbs away from the colliery in October 1979 towards the exchange sidings with coal for the now-decimated Lanarkshire steel industry. On withdrawal, this particular locomotive was to find a new home at the Scottish Railway Preservation Society's Bo'ness & Kinneil Railway. *Bob Avery*

Above:
Pounds (Shipowners & Ship Breakers) Ltd at Cairn Ryan, Wigtownshire owned this 0-6-0PT (works No 2614/1940) when photographed on 29 May 1967. Supplied new to HM Dockyard Rosyth *No 4 Fife*, served until June 1961 when it departed for Pounds. Despite lasting until the preservation era was well underway this Bagnall-built locomotive was not to survive.
Geoff Lumb

Right:
Bedlay Colliery, Glenboig, Lanarkshire, just north of Coatbridge, was the last to use steam in Scotland. Built in 1909 Hudswell Clarke 0-6-0T, NCB No 9, is seen here propelling empty wagons towards the pit head in February 1979. Today the engine is a static exhibit at Summerlee Heritage Park, Coatbridge.
Tom Heavyside

Far right:
With a rake of empty mineral wagons in tow this 1909-built 0-6-0T shunts at the NCB's Glenboig Colliery in February 1979.
Derek Huntriss